Sales:
How to influence people, persuade, and close the sale

Simon Roche

Finicky Inc.
New York

About me

Motivational Coffee
Hi, my name is Simon Roche, Founder of "Finicky.us"
and also the author to many entrepreneurial and self-
help books.

I have seen that I was different since I was a kid.
When other kids wanted to play, I wanted to be
productive and better myself. Not to say that I didn't
play on my free time, I just didn't play longer than I
needed. I always set my expectations out of my reach
and I truly hope that my readers do the same. I have
visited many companies during my career and I can
say that I have learned more than if I were to have
worked for a company.

As a thank you for considering my book, I will provide
you with one of my many experiences while visiting a
friend at Google. My friend who was previously the
"Strategic Partner Lead" at Google has had many
accomplish through his career and no longer works at
Google. We became friends in our marketing course
and have still kept in contact.

He gave me a tip about the process of hiring people
for my company. During the selection process, he
weaves out many strong candidates. Why? Simply

because they aren't smarter than me, the interviewer. He explains that if you want a good company, then you surround yourself with average brains that just want to get by. At Google, we don't want average, we want the smartest. Smart people hire smarter people and that's how Google is still on top of its industry. He stated, "I want to hire someone who is smarter than me, works better than me, and is more innovative than me. That way I will be happy when they take my position, as I move on to another chapter in my life"

Through my books, I will share many of my unique experiences and will provide you with mistakes that I have made myself as an entrepreneur.

Words from the Author

Before you start reading this book, I will need you to keep a thought in mind.

"To be able to sacrifice what you are, for who you will become"

In other words, if you put aside your excuses, you will get the results you have always wanted. It's time to make a decision. You can choose to stay the way you are or you can decide to take steps towards change. No one is stopping you from where you want to go, the only person that is stopping you is YOU. Remind yourself every day of who you want to be, and remember to make the right decisions towards your goal. One way to keep your goals set is by checking up on yourself at the end of each week. Set a goal for 2 pounds each week, and by the end of the month you will have cut 8 pounds. Keep your short-term goals small so that it is achievable, but keep your long-term goals big, so that there is no ceiling towards your success.

Introduction

Knowing your way around making a sale can be a very handy skill to have. Whether you're a salesman/woman or just a regular person off the street, possessing the skill to sell can highly benefit you. However, before we get started, it's important to understand that marketing plays a very large role in sales. For this reason, the "sales field" is always noted as Sales & Marketing, or just S&M.

The Sales & Marketing field consists of three main pillars. A lack of one of the pillars could cause a big decrease in your sales, which means a loss of revenue and profit. The first pillar is obviously sales. This pillar's primary focus is bringing revenue to the company, which is done by reaching out to the customer and convincing them that your product or service is exactly what they are looking for. The second pillar would be marketing, which is creating a sort of desire out of your clients or customers. It includes the pricing of the product/service, the looks, packaging, logo, etc. The third and final pillar is innovation, or the future of what you're selling. Innovation includes the long-term strategies for your product/service, which are targeted towards getting your clients/customers to come back to you time and time again.

In this book, you will learn how to efficiently make a sale from start to end. The primary focus will be on the sales department, but it's important to keep the marketing and innovation departments in mind. The sales you make will help pay for the costs of the other two departments. However, with good marketing and innovation, sales will become a lot easier to come by.

The truth is, everybody is a salesman/woman. You use your selling skills everyday, whether it's at work, on the street, talking to your parents or even to yourself. Strengthening your sales skill starts with the preparation of the sale, continues with reaching out to the client/customer, then closing the sale.

Another good skill of a salesman/woman is bouncing back after a sale fails. By staying positive, that lost sale won't feel like that bad of a loss. Lastly, this book will point out a few common mistakes that are made while making sales. By avoiding these mistakes, your sales will go a lot smoother and more successful.

Chapter 1: The Everyday Salesman

As I stated before, selling is relevant in pretty much everything. Whether you're selling a company's product, selling your services to someone, or simply just trying to get your friend to try the newest gum flavor, your selling skills are going to be tested.

Throughout this chapter, you will be introduced to some of the major careers and moments when you're sales skill will be put to the test. If you notice that you find yourself in many of the same predicaments, then it's apparent that you will need to have a strong selling skill. If not, then don't be discouraged because you can still benefit from adding this skill.

Sales In The Workforce

Let's be honest, almost every job or career that you have will require some type of selling. First, let's talk about the traditional retail job. If you work retail, then you were most likely hired as a sales associate, which means you are responsible for driving sales to your company. Here's an activity to try:

Next time you take a trip to the mall, go inside each and every store in there. The chances of a worker coming up to you once you step foot in the store are very high. This is because that worker is now trying to

persuade you to buy something. Almost every store is
going to have a sales associate, whether it's
American Eagle, Victoria's Secret, Sears or Target.

Next, let's move on to people who sell "big-ticket items." For the most part, these are people highly experienced when it comes to selling something face-to-face. You will find these salesmen/women attempting to sell you a car, a house, a financial service, securities, etc. Instead of being called sales associates, these people are often titled as consultants because they hold endless knowledge about the item or service they are selling. (Yes, this is why they almost always get you to buy something)

Lastly, I just want to give you a couple more examples of some other jobs that require you to sell. Telemarketers are a perfect example of workers who use selling skills throughout their workday. Since they are forced to complete all their sales over the phone, it takes a lot more skill than your face-to-face sales. More examples include travel agents, insurance agents, promoters and demonstrators.

Sales Elsewhere

Consultative selling, which is when the salesperson learns about someone else's needs in order to figure out the best product for them, is the kind of selling that you will find most common outside of the workplace. With consultative selling, you start by asking questions to get a better feel for what someone needs. Here's a quick example of when you could find consultative selling outside of the workforce:

Mom: What should we get to eat, son?
Son: Depends, what are you in the mood for?
Mom: I was thinking something quick. Maybe fast-food?
Son: Fast food sounds good to me. I heard Burger King brought back their Chicken Fries and I haven't had it in so long. Would you be interested in going there?
Mom: I don't know, let me think about it.
Son: They also have a variety of salads and chicken sandwiches to choose from. Does that interest you more?
Mom: That actually sounds perfect. Let's go to Burger King.

As you can see, when the son heard that his mother was hungry, he first asked what she was in the mood for. This narrowed down the list of possible places to eat, based on his mother's wants and needs. He then pitched an idea, but knew it would have to take some selling for it to be a success. After a little persuasion, the son closed the sale and he went to Burger King with his mother.

As you read deeper into this book, you will notice that there are several different methods of selling.

However, they all work with the same core values. These values are to be used before, during and after you make a sale. The first core value is preparation.

Chapter Two: Preparing For A Sale

Before you jump into a sale, it's important that you have an expert understanding of what you are selling, who you will be selling to and what they will be looking for. The preparation process is the seller's opportunity to learn as much as they can about whatever they are selling, whether it's an item, service, project, product or a job. It also gives them that chance to prepare their sales pitch, making sure it appeals to the target audience.

Since the preparation process is such an important value when selling, you will most likely be spending a lot of your time doing just that. There's a lot of work for you to do, but to make it simpler, I've created a good starter's list on how to prepare for a sale.

By following these helpful tips, you will no doubt be ready to sell when that moment comes.

- **Identify audience.** Before entering a sale, you should know who you are selling to. This will make a huge difference in your sales pitch and your approach. If it's a single person, who is it? Are they a male or female? What's their approximate age going to be? If it's a group of people, how old are they going to be? Try to get as much information on your target audience as possible.

- **Customer's needs.** Another thing you should know about your audience is what they need. If you work at a fragrance store, then research what you have to offer them. If you're selling houses, think about the kind of house the CUSTOMER wants. Knowing the customer's needs will help you figure out what they need quicker. Likewise, if there are any promotions or deals that your company is offering, could that be a reason that they came to you? If you're running a sale on body lotion, then that is most likely the reason they came into your store.
- **Language.** Another important thing to consider before hitting the sales is the language you should use. Will you be talking to kids or adults? Are they serious businessmen or are they comedians? Chances are, you're going to talk differently when trying to sell a kid a toy, than when you sell an adult a house. If you're talking to a group of finance people, you should probably include numbers and charts into your pitch. Since everyone speaks differently, it's good to know what kind of language you should be using when selling.
- **What are you selling?** Obviously, it would be smart to know what you are selling before you try and sell it. You will most likely be much more successful if you do some research before-hand. Are you selling a product? If so, what kind of product? What are it's uses? It's

pros? It's cons? Are you selling an idea? A service? If so, do you know how much it will cost, what features will come with it, your availability, etc.? The point is, try and learn as much as you can about what you are selling. That way when a customer has questions, you are already prepared with an answer. Preparation leads to credibility when it comes time to sell.

- **Know the benefits.** Any features that come with a product or service are going to be a good way to market whatever you are selling. However, the customer is only going to be focused on one thing: What's in it for me? After you've educated yourself on the features of what you are selling, it's time to learn the benefits it will bring to your customer. For example, if you are selling body lotion, then a feature would be that it contains moisturizing aloe. However, the benefit of that feature is that your hands stay moisturized for a long period of time. By giving benefits to your customer, instead of just features, you will build a more emotional connection with them. This will lead to more sales, due to the gained trust from the customer.

- **Your "pitch."** A sales pitch is your presentation of what you are selling. If you're a real estate agent, your pitch would be given at an open house. Your pitch will bring together everything you have learned throughout the preparation process. Once put together, be sure to practice that pitch over and over again. The more comfortable you feel giving your pitch, the more the customer will believe that they should buy from you.

You've studied all that you could study on your product, service, idea, etc. Can you turn that knowledge into action, though? Hopefully, because that's what the next step contains. If you are ready to hit the sales floor, or the telephone, or however you are selling, then what are you waiting around for?

Chapter Three: Get To Know Your Client

Now that you are ready to get sales, it's time to put that knowledge to work. Your first order of business is getting to know your client. In order to successfully give the customer what they need, you have to understand what that need is. How are you going to get that answer? By approaching them and asking! The only way you are going to get to know your client is if you express an interest in doing so.

For this chapter, let's say that you are a sales associate at the body care store, Bath & Body Works. Your main purpose is to bring the company sales by connecting with the customer and satisfying their needs.

Below is a list of helpful tips that will make your pitch a lot more successful. Remember to stay on your toes and be ready for any questions or concerns the customer has.

- **Approach Customer.** Once you see a customer walk into your store, the first thing you should do is greet them. It doesn't have to be too complex, just something simple, like "Hello. How are you?" or "Welcome!" Whatever you do, just remember to maintain a positive attitude and stay friendly. Smile as you greet people, have energy in your voice, keep a good posture. This is your first impression that you are sending to your customer, so it's important not to screw it up.

- **Begin Conversation.** After greeting them, it's smart to not jump directly into the sale. Be subtle, start a conversation. If you like the shoes they are wearing, compliment them. See how their day is going, comment about the weather, anything! Basically, start the conversation with small talk. It's a good ice breaker before you begin to persuade them to buy something. It's also a good way to form a bond or connection with them.
- **Ask Questions.** Once the ice has been broken with your customer, start asking them what brought them in today. If you're a telemarketer, start to ask questions that relate to what you are selling. A good way to start this off is by asking, "Is there anything I can help you find?" For the most part, the customer will know what they are looking for. If that's the case, then listen to their response carefully. This is where all of the knowledge from the preparation process comes to use. You have to be ready with a response for what this customer says. The key is to keep asking them questions until you figure out what the best product is for that customer. In this case, ask them what their favorite scent is, what kind of body care item they were looking for.

In the event that the customer says, "I'm okay, I'm just going to look around," after you ask them if you can help them find anything, then stay friendly. Giving them attitude will only upset them, which is never good. In that case, just say, "Not a problem. Let me know if you need any help." If you want to, leave them with any promotions that you are currently honoring.

- **Reveal.** Now that you know what your customer is looking for, it's time to show them what that is. If they are looking for a body lotion, bring them to the body lotions. If they have a favorite scent, show them what you offer in that scent. If the customer doesn't like what you pointed out, ask them why. This will give you an even better understanding of what they need. The key to this is to keep working with the customer until they reach satisfaction. Remember, the customer is always right and you should always cater to their needs.

- **Body Language.** The body language you present to the customer is just as important as the body language they present to you. If you keep a monotone voice and look slouched and tired, the customer isn't going to be fully engaged in your pitch. This is why it's always important to keep good posture and keep a positive and friendly tone of voice.

Similar to that, you need to pay attention to the body language of your audience, customer or client. If they are showing signs of frustration with you, boredom or impatience, then you should probably consider wrapping things up or moving on to the next part of the pitch.

When selling, it's important to avoid making it look like just that. Instead, make them feel like they're being helped. It will help you build a more emotional connection with them, which will ultimately allow you to sell to them more effectively. If you feel that they are ready to buy, then go ahead and attempt to close the sale.

Chapter Four: Closing The Sale Correctly

You've gotten a customer or client interested in what you're selling, but does that necessarily mean that they are going to buy it? The answer to that question is: No. The sale isn't over until they've committed to buying from you and you see the revenue go into your business. Until then, you still have persuading and bonding to do!

In the last chapter, you were a retail sales associate. If that were the case, then closing the sale would include ringing them up at the cash register and bagging up their product. However, we are going to switch things up. For this chapter, you are going to be a real estate agent that has just completed their pitch to their client. You are now ready to close the sale.

While closing the sale, keep these helpful tips in mind.

- **Questions, concerns, comments.** After you have finished your pitch, allow your client a moment to ask you any questions he might have about, in this case, the house. This includes any concerns they have with the house, comments, doubts, anything. This is their chance to get anything off their chest for you to answer, so be ready to give them that answer, whatever it may be.

- **Friendliness.** This rule doesn't change just because you are certain they are going to buy. You must remain friendly and courteous to your client throughout the whole sale. Yes, even if the client has a rude comment or a serious question/concern. Make them feel comfortable and relaxed before giving them the answer. Also, you will come off a lot more friendly if you continue asking them if they have any other questions until they say "no."
- **Commitment.** After all of the questions are out of the way, it's time to get some sort of commitment out of them. If you're a telemarketer, see if they are ready to buy. If you're a sales associate, ask if they are ready to be rung up. However, keep in mind that this doesn't always have to be the end of the sale. Their commitment could be to come in two days from now to further discuss the product, idea or service. The main focus should be on getting some kind of commitment from the client. In the event that they do commit to come back for another visit, it will buy you some time to further examine their concerns and how you can accommodate them appropriately.
- **Close.** Now that you have a commitment from them, close the sale. Whatever process you have to go through to close it, do it. Any signatures, paperwork, money transactions, agreements, etc.

Lastly, be prepared to be tested. Some customers will be difficult, some will be rude and some will just be straight-up hard to sell. When that moment comes, it's your job to stay cool and handle it professionally. Whether it's an objection to your pitch, a problem with a product or just a failed sale all-together, you need to know how to handle it.

Chapter Five: Objections and Failures

As a salesperson, you need to be prepared for the worst while expecting the best. The reality of selling is that not everyone is going leave a buyer. Some are going to leave empty-handed, some will leave disappointed or mad, and some will leave with less than what you were hoping for. However, it's important to stay friendly and positive no matter what the situation is. If you stay professional, then the customer will leave happy even if they don't get what they want.

In this chapter we are going to talk about two things that are bound to happen during your selling ventures: objections and failures. Read below for tips on how to handle those two situations in a way that keeps everyone happy.

Objections

The reason we are going to talk about objections first is because these aren't a definite "no" from the customer or client. In fact, objections can actually help your cause. They show that the audience you are selling to isn't afraid to ask questions or express their concerns that they may have. The point is, embrace objections for what they are, a reassurance of why your customer should buy from you.

The only difficult thing about objections is that you can never know what they are going to be. Everyone is going to have their own opinions, which will cause everyone to have their own problems or questions about it. For this reason, you will need to be quick on your feet with your responses. Being ready for a question means that you are quick with a response, but also that your response fully answers their question.

One tip that will help you look more professional during these types of interactions is to always answer with a question. Not only will this give the customer a chance to elaborate their question for your, but will also give you a little bit of time to think of a response. Here's an example:

Customer: My problem with buying a coffee machine is that it is too expensive.

Associate: Yes, it is expensive. However, if you don't buy it, then you will spend much more money every morning by going to the cafe an ordering a coffee. So, when thinking long-term, don't you think this coffee machine is a much smarter choice?

As you can see, the question showed the customer that you were willing to work with them to find a solution to their problem, or in this case a justification. In the end, you addressed her concern, you reassured them that your product was right for them, and then you moved on from it positively.

Failures

When your job or career is in the sales field, you need to know that you are going to have moments of failure. Not everyone is going to buy what you try to sell and that's just the reality of it. However, it's important that you handle those situations appropriately and professionally. Just because the sale failed this time, doesn't mean that they won't come back again in the future. This is why you must leave them with a positive attitude no matter what, or else that return may never come.

One tip to leave a failed buyer with a good impression is to remain polite and friendly throughout your entire interaction with them. Here's an example of how you can word it:

"I'm sorry we couldn't find what you were looking for today. Hopefully we can be of more help in the future. We'll see you next time. Have a good night!"

The apology lets the customer know that you are sincere and will leave them with a positive attitude as they walk out the door. Also, since most salesmen/women don't back out after a sale fails, they will be surprised when you do. This will likely cause them to be more receptive to you the next time they see you.

If you're a real estate agent and the house you showed a potential buyer wasn't a good fit for them, you can handle it a different way. Instead of closing the sale, you can keep it open by offering to show them another house. This is why it is sometimes good to have several different plans of attack. Now that you know this house wasn't a good fit, you can select one that is based on the gained knowledge from the first house. The only downside to this is that the customer could get restless with you and frustrated. This should be avoided, so don't go overboard with your customers/clients.

Chapter Six: Common Selling Mistakes

When put out into the sales battlefield, there are certain things you should refrain from doing. Listed below is a list of common mistakes that salesmen/women often find themselves doing. In doing so, they are hurting their chances of making that sale.

- Many times, sales people will find themselves talking instead of listening. During a potential sale, the customer or client should be doing most of the talking. Meanwhile, the seller should be listening and thinking of how they could best serve their needs. If you find yourself in this predicament, then you will notice the customer growing bored of your pitch. This should be a red flag to move on to something else and get your audience engaged.
- Another mistake commonly made is when you presume instead of asking questions. By presuming what the customer needs, you are essentially selling them something they most likely don't want. By doing this, your sales numbers will drop dramatically. To save you from this, always ask questions. This will ensure that you know what the customer wants and will lead to them leaving satisfied customers.

- If a customer or client makes a statement or comment about your product or one of its features, it doesn't necessarily require an answer. Many sales people get defensive and start justifying why it is the way it is. Instead, you should resort to asking questions to find out what you could do to help.

- Another mistake many people make is not letting go of a customer when the sale is obviously dead. So many salesmen/women spend much of their time on clients who they aren't going to get a response from. Instead, focus your energy on making new clients. If someone doesn't seem interested, don't chase after them. You should only chase after customers/clients that are worth chasing.

- Also, try not to jump to conclusions while attempting to make a sale. During a sale, many people will assume something without having the necessary data and information to back it up. To avoid this, keep asking questions until you are positive that your assumption is correct. By jumping to too many conclusions, the customer will get frustrated with you. When that happens, you can pretty much kiss the sale goodbye.

- As I talked about in Chapter Two, preparation is one of the main values to selling. Without it, you can become overwhelmed with everything that goes on during a sale. A common mistake is that people don't take that preparation time seriously. Without research, you will have nothing to talk about and will have difficulty establishing a bond or connection with the customer/client. In addition, research will reassure you that the customer/client is a good fit for you. That way, you don't end up wasting time on someone who isn't interested in what you have to offer.

- Another mistake that is seen a lot is when someone spends too much time with small talk. Small talk is only good for a certain amount of time before you need to start selling. The reasoning behind it is that the customer isn't only interested in building a relationship with you, but they are also interested in hearing what you have to offer.

- One last mistake that is commonly made is when salesmen/women are too optimistic. Yes, it's okay to be positive and welcoming. However, if you take it too far, you will often be blinded when the customer start showing signs that they're slipping away. When you miss those signs, you can upset or frustrate the client/customer which will lead to a lost or failed sale.

Conclusion

In conclusion, I would like to summarize everything we've gone over in this book. It might seem like a lot to take in, but it's not. If you think about it, everyone sells everyday. It's a very common skill used that is important to society.

All of the background knowledge that comes when selling something is learned throughout the preparation process. This is where you learn as much as you can about the service you offer, the product you're selling or the idea you are pitching. The knowledge will help you later during the actual sales engagement.

Once you're fully prepared, you're ready to put your sales pitch to work. There are a lot of things to keep in mind while selling. If you recall, one of those things is being friendly, patient and polite. Another one is to refrain from talking too much by asking the customer or client questions. The sales pitch is your opportunity to show the customer why you are the best fit for them. By keeping the customer or client happy, you can ensure a smooth pitch.

Remember, before attempting to close a sale, make sure the customer is ready. This can be assured by asking them if they have any additional questions, comments or concerns. If not, then proceed with the closing of the sale. Whether you need to ring them up or go through paperwork, get it done.

In the event that you encounter an objection or a failed sale, it's important to keep your positive attitude and professional manners. Stepping out of those zones will cause more frustration on your customer's end, which will only complicate the sale more.

The last piece of advice I'm going to leave you with is to have fun with it. Think about it as if you were on the other end of the process. If you were the buyer, customer or client, how would you like the salesman/woman to act? How would you expect them to address your questions and concerns? The answers to those questions should resemble the way you currently act as a salesman/woman. By creating a fun and friendly environment for the customer, you can be sure of a successful sale, a healthy business relationship and a recurring customer.

Thank you for reading this book! Good luck with your sales!

BIG Bonus from the Author

I want you to thank yourself for wanting to change and I
hope you walk away inspired or smarter.
As you read on you will find tips used by entrepreneurs,
and motivational thoughts that come from coaches and
entrepreneurs themselves. Have Fun and good luck with
your endeavors. Before moving on, I just want to remind
you that we are all born on this earth as equals. Some may
have more support than others, but we can only
characterize ourselves by our own actions. In other words,
everyone in this world has potential hidden in a box. Some
choose to find a way to open it, and some just leave it there.
Think about this and try to figure out who you are.
Some may be okay living an average life, but then there are
also others who constantly look for better.

Life Hacking Tips Used by the Entrepreneurs!

Coffee Nap

Didn't Get Enough Sleep Last Night?
Take A Mid-day Coffee Nap.

- TOTD #1

Health is Wealth

This method provided is called, "Caffeine Nap", where you drink a cup of coffee and nap for 15 minutes. The 15 minutes gives you time to rest and allows the caffeine to travel through your gastro-intestinal tract. This will provide you with a refreshing reboot by the time you wake up. But don't go over the 15-20 minutes limit or else you'll wake up in a sleepy state.

Plan the Night Before

Plan Out Your Day The Night Before.
Don't Waste Your Mornings
Preparing Your Work Schedule.

-TOTD # 2

Health is Wealth

You heard of this before, you can either work hard or work smart. It's your choice. There's nothing wrong about working hard, but what's the point of working hard if the results are not there. You need to work smart and change up your routine so that your work is actually effective. Tonight before you go to bed, plan out your work for the next day so that you don't waste time in the morning. Don't waste your mornings on planning out what you want to work on as you are wasting your brains fuel. Your brain is packed with fuel from last night's rest, so go use it on something productive. Don't be like the majority of people who sit on their desk wondering what they need to do. Hope this helps!

Acknowledge Your Accomplishments, But....

You have one win in your hand, but that's not enough. It's not time to celebrate just yet. This is only a small win towards your goal. If you celebrate now, you might just lose the fire that you've always had in you to pursue your dreams. So when you reach a goal, recognize it. Please do so as it will be your source of motivation. The motivation that tells you, maybe it is possible. Maybe this dream isn't out of my reach. Just remember to set your goals high and when you do reach them, set them even higher the next time.

Must Always Take a Break

Remember to Take a Break From Work
-TOTD #4

Health is Wealth

Most of us work for a living, and sometimes we work so hard that we feel too tired to spend time with the people we love. Just remember that our work will always change, but our family will always be there. On another thought, we need to take breaks during excessive periods of work, so that we can replenish our thoughts. Take a walk and get some fresh air.

Are You Committed?

Are you interested or are you committed to achieving your current goals? Most may ask, what is the difference? If you have interest in fulfilling your goals, then you will complete your task and never look back. In other words, you will do things the same way as how most people do it. However, if you are committed to your situation, then you will find yourself working more than you need to, and trying to improve your current goals, although they are already good enough. Successful entrepreneurs are successful because they have a purpose behind their tasks, it is more than just interest. So just ask yourself, are you interested or are you committed to what you are currently doing.

There Should Never Be a Plan "B"

If You Concentrate And Exploit The Weaknesses Of Plan A, There Will Be No Need For A Plan B.

Health is Wealth

You've all heard of Plan B's. They are there to back you up just in case Plan A doesn't work. But what's the point of spending half your time on Plan A and half your time on Plan B. Instead, use your time to focus solely on Plan A so that you can perfect it. A perfect plan is better than two average plans. I've always grown up being told "If you do it right the first time, you won't have to do it a second time". So why do it a second time, you're just wasting energy. Perfect your 1st attempt so that you can move on and accomplish other things in life.

Become a Warrior

Rough Times Are Going To Come,
But They Have Not Come To Stay.
They Have Come To Pass.

Health is Wealth

It's not like we're never going to get hurt in life. And it's not like these episodes are meant to devastate us. These harsh times are just the flow of life and everyone gets them, we just need to do our part and accept them. It may sound easy but it really isn't. To accept tragedy or a mishap in your life is going to be hard because we're humans. We're emotional and that's understandable, but what about life. Life isn't going to wait for you, it's like a train with no brakes. The Sun is still going to shine, and the Moon is still going to glow. So try not to mourn for too long. These hard times are bound to come, but they have not come to stay. They have come to pass.

A Forgotten Lifestyle

Live Simply,
So That Others
May Simply Live

Health is Wealth
healthiswealth.us

This is probably going to be my favorite for a while. Live simply, so that others may simply live. A simple saying that would do wonders for the world. In a world where capitalism is King, we often get carried away by lavish lifestyles that we envy of others. There's nothing wrong with treating yourself after a hard day's work. It's just that sometimes we become a bit too selfish. There are many people around us that aren't even able to even eat 3 times a day, and here we are complaining about getting the newest gadgets. Our job to live simply is not going to kill us. We may miss out on getting a few designer handbags or suits, but at the end of the day those funds will allow the unfortunate to live another day.

Stop Waiting and Just Do It

You Cannot Escape
The Responsibilities Of Tomorrow
By Evading It Today.

Health is Wealth
healthiswealth.us

I'll do it later. For some reason we only feel obliged to start
working when the deadline is near. Maybe you just need
pressure to start working. We all put off work until later
and our work becomes faulty when we're done. No time left
to correct your mistakes. But that's not how successful
people succeed and we need to instill in our minds to
organize your workload so that you don't do last minute
work.

You Are Only One Person, But...

The Only Way Change
Will Ever Happen, Is If We Speak Up.
Our Words Are Powerful, Lets Make An Impact.

Health is Wealth
healthiswealth.us

This was always my problem. I'm guilty of the, "but I'm just one person" crime. I'm so used to assuming that other people are going to make an effort to change their surroundings that I suppose my input wouldn't make a difference. So what if you're just one person. If you're making a change and people around you see it, then they'll be inspired to make the change with you. You are never just one. There may be many others in the room who have the same idea as you, but are not confident enough to share. Stand up and speak your mind so that confidence may grow in them too. The only way change will ever happen, is if we speak up. Our words are powerful, let's make an impact. Don't ever think of yourself as just one.

My Dream Never Faded. Your Doubts Just made it More Clear to Me

They Asked Him, How Did He Do It?
He Replied,
There Was No One Here
To Tell Me I Couldn't Do It.

Health is Wealth

Are you sure? No one has ever done it before, so how will you do it? It's Impossible.

Well that's not new. People telling you what's possible and what's impossible. But what do they know. They don't know how much time and effort you put in every day and night into your work. If they tell you that it's impossible, let it fuel your fire. Proving people wrong was always a hobby of mine. So go out there and work. And when that day comes, you could tell your doubters that it was always possible.

Even if no one sees it for you, you must see it for yourself. And just like that you are on the road to success.

How's Your Willpower?

Stop setting goals and stopping half way. Sometimes we get inspired and decide to dream big. And after the next day the inspiration is gone and we decide to quit. The problem is not that we have set your goals too high. There's no such thing as setting your goals too high. The problem is us. If we don't want it bad enough, then we will be like the majority of people who start something and then say it's getting nowhere. Well don't expect results to come in just a couple of days, this is a long term commitment. We have to be committed to what we do in order to get far. We can start and end half way, but what does that really say about our willpower. You are only as good as your weakest day.

We Used to Dream a Lot

When We Were Kids, We Saw Things Differently.
In The Simplest Things Around Us, We Imagined
Endless Possibilities.

Health is Wealth

Back then we used to tie a towel around our neck and jump off our beds only to soar for a couple of seconds. But those couple of seconds were enough to allow us to feel like superheroes. We turned that towel into a cape and it gave us an identity. When we were kids, we saw things differently. In the simplest things around us, we imagined endless possibilities. Who would have known that a chunk of metal would help us fly around the world? That's absurd right? It's hard to imagine an airplane from looking at a chunk of metal. As we grow older we slowly push our imaginations aside, and that towel that used to help us fly is just a rag to us now. We've grown up in a world filled with pessimists, whom only know how to provide doubts into our imaginations. It's hard to be innovative when we have so much doubts in our own ideas. So just let those imaginations come back and give them another chance. You'll never know where those imaginations will take you.

G.R.I.N.D.

Sometimes I feel like I'm not making any progress toward my goals and it frightens me. My dreams and goals are still there, but I have my doubts like any human would. So today I turned on my speakers and Asher Roth was on. It was only then that I realized that I was doing it all wrong. My goal was to work hard so that I could buy my parents stuff that they would be happy to have. I wanted them to be happy. I wanted them to know that in the near future, their working hours would be lessened and that I would bombard them with gifts.

But it wasn't until today, that I realize how faulty my goals were. I was so focused on spending time on work for a better future that I nearly forgot about spending time with my parents in the present. Spending money on my parents can come a little later, but for now it's about spending time with the people you love. Happiness isn't not about getting what you want all the time, it's about loving what you have. So get ready, it's a new day.

Appreciate What You Have!

Appreciate What You Have
&
You'll End Up Having More

Health is Wealth

Today we are so focused with getting new things that we neglect what we already have. We look forward to creating new relationships, and leave behind the relationships we already have. Instead of trying to fix the problems in our current situations, we look for something new as a solution, but at the end of the day we are just dragging out the problem. So let's fix something today, before looking elsewhere. When a friendship is confronted with problems, they settle the problem with each other and grow stronger together.

Stuck in Your Comfort Zone?

The First Step To Success? Refuse To Be A Captive Of Your Environment.

Health is Wealth
healthiswealth.us

You say you want to be healthy. You say you want to be rich. But are you doing anything towards these goals. Surrounding yourself with a room full of junk food is not going to help. Neither is hanging around people who don't believe in working hard. You need to get out of your old environment and go find a new one. Stop being trapped in the misery that is around you. Go meet new friends that actually care about the wellness of their body and people who set new goals every week. Once you are in their environment, you'll find yourself trying to work as hard as or even harder than them. Place yourself in a healthy environment, but first you have to leave your old one.

Thank you for taking the time to read this book and may you always have a perfectly balanced life. If you haven't already read my author's description before purchasing this book, you would know that I am also the founder of Finicky. The images provided by the book come from my website, "Finicky.us"

Preview of "Public Speaking: 7 Essentials Steps Used by Top Entrepreneurs"

You may purchase this book by clicking here
Or by using this link http://amzn.to/1dsxVg9

The feeling of nervousness or stage-fright when presenting to an audience is perfectly normal. Even the best public speakers still get nervous. This is a part of being human, we are wired to be worried about our reputation and public speaking is a threat to us. In psychological terms, our fight or flight responses comes into play and our body starts feeling different.

Before I go on any further, I would just like to tell you that the fears of public speaking are not to be overcome, we need to adapt to our public speaking environment. I would like you to keep this in mind as you continue to read on.

Before considering talking in public there are some things you must be aware of. The first thing you should do before speaking in public is to find out who you are and what you need.

The feedback you will receive after speaking in public is relevant for what you are going to do next. You should always meditate and answer these questions: Who am I? What do I want? What do I need?

www.ingramcontent.com/pod-product-compliance
Lightning Source LLC
Chambersburg PA
CBHW071007180526
45168CB00003B/1322